3 Beloved Tales

Little RED RIDING HOOD

Stories Around the World

by Jessica Gunderson

PICTURE WINDOW BOOKS
a capstone imprint

What Is a Fairy Tale?

Once upon a time, before the age of books, people gathered to tell stories. They told tales of fairies and magic, princes and witches. Ideas of love, jealousy, kindness, and luck filled the stories. Some provided lessons. Others just entertained. Most did both! These fairy tales passed from neighbor to neighbor, village to village, land to land. As the stories spun across seas and over mountains, details changed to fit each culture. A poisoned slipper became a poisoned ring. A king became a sultan. A wolf became a tiger.

Over time, fairy tales were collected and written down. Around the world today, people of all ages love to read or hear these timeless stories. For many years to come, fairy tales will continue to live happily ever after in our imaginations.

Little Red Riding Hood
A German Fairy Tale

illustrated by Colleen Madden

Once upon a time, there lived a sweet girl named Little Red Riding Hood. She got her name from the red velvet riding hood she wore. It was a gift from her adoring grandmother.

One day the girl's mother gave her a loaf of bread and a bottle of wine. She said, "Take these to your grandmother. She is ill and weak. And don't stray from the path."

Little Red Riding Hood set off through the woods. Along the way, she met a wolf. She didn't know he was a wicked beast, so she wasn't afraid.

"What are you carrying in that basket?" the wolf asked.

"Bread and wine for my grandmother," the girl answered.

"Where does she live?" asked the wolf.

"In a cottage under three big oak trees," said the girl.

The wolf grinned. *She is a tender young thing,* he thought. *She will taste better than the old grandmother. I must be crafty ...*

The wolf walked alongside Little Red Riding Hood for a while. Then he said, "Let's race to your grandmother's house and see who gets there first! I'll go this way, and you cut through the trees."

"What a grand idea!" the girl exclaimed. She left the path and ran into the woods.

The wolf reached Grandmother's house first and knocked on the door. "It's Little Red Riding Hood," he said in a sweet voice.

"Come in, dear," said Grandmother.

The wolf opened the door and swallowed the poor old woman. He put on her spare cap, nightgown, and glasses and got into bed to wait.

Little Red Riding Hood soon arrived. She called, "Hello!" and pulled back the bed covers. The girl thought her grandmother looked very strange. "Grandmother, what big ears you have!" she said.

"The better to hear you with," said the wolf.

"What big eyes you have!" she exclaimed.

"The better to see you with."

"What big hands you have!"

"The better to hug you with."

"Grandmother, what big teeth you have!" Little Red Riding Hood cried.

"The better to eat you with!" the wolf snarled. He jumped out of bed and swallowed the poor girl.

Now the wolf felt full. He lay down on the bed and began to snore very loudly.

A hunter passed by and heard the wolf's snores. He saw the wolf on the bed.

He knew the wolf must have eaten the grandmother, so
he grabbed a pair of shears and cut open the wolf's belly.
Out jumped Little Red Riding Hood and her grandmother.

Little Red Riding Hood ran outside and fetched some large stones. She and the hunter filled the wolf's belly with them. When the wolf awoke, he tried to run off. But the stones were so heavy, he fell down dead. The hunter skinned the wolf and took the pelt home with him.

Grandmother ate the bread and drank the wine Little Red Riding Hood had brought and felt better. Little Red Riding Hood told herself she'd never again stray from the path in the woods.

The False Grandmother

An Italian Fairy Tale   illustrated by Eva Montanari

One day a mother was making bread. She told her little girl to run to her grandmother's house and borrow the flour sifter. The girl packed a snack of ring-shaped cakes and bread with oil. Then she set out.

When she reached the river, she asked, "River, will you let me cross?"

The river liked to spin ring-shaped cakes in his whirlpools. He answered, "Yes, if you give me your cakes."

The girl tossed the cakes into the river, and the river let her cross.

The girl then arrived at a gate. "Gate, will you let me through?"

The gate's hinges were rusty, and the bread with oil would loosen them. The gate answered, "Yes, if you give me your bread with oil."

The little girl did, and the gate opened.

When the girl reached her grandmother's house, she found the door locked. "Grandmother, let me in!" she called.

"I'm sick in bed," Grandmother said. "I'll pull you up through the window." She lowered a rope so the girl could climb up.

The room was dark. The girl couldn't see that in the bed lay an ogress, not her grandmother. The ogress had gobbled up the grandmother.

"Mother wants the sifter," the girl said.

"It's too late. Come to bed now," the ogress said. "I'll give you the sifter tomorrow."

The little girl crawled into bed beside the ogress. "Grandmother, why are your hands so hairy?" she asked.

"From wearing too many rings," the ogress answered.

"Why is your chest so hairy?"

"From wearing too many necklaces."

"Why are your hips so hairy?"

"From wearing my corset too tight."

Then the little girl felt the ogress' tail. She knew her grandmother, hairy or not, had never had a tail. At once she realized the woman was an ogress.

"Grandmother, I have to go to the bathroom," the girl said.

"Go to the barn below," said the ogress. She tied a rope around the girl and let her down through the trapdoor.

The moment the girl reached the ground, she untied the rope. She re-tied it around a heavy nanny goat.

"OK! Pull me back up," she called and then ran away.

The ogress pulled and pulled. Up came the nanny goat! The ogress jumped out of bed and chased after the little girl.

The girl reached the gate with the ogress at her heels.
"Don't let her through, Gate!" the ogress yelled.

"Of course I'll let her through," the gate answered.
"She gave me bread with oil."

When the girl reached the river, the ogress yelled, "River, don't let her cross!"

"Of course I'll let her cross," the river answered. "She gave me ring-shaped cakes."

When the ogress tried to cross the river, the waters rose quickly. The ogress was swept away by the current. The little girl stood on the riverbank, making faces at the ogress.

Grandaunt Tiger
A Taiwanese Fairy Tale illustrated by Carolina Farías

One day a mother went on an errand and left her two daughters home alone. She warned them not to open the door to anyone. "Especially not to Grandaunt Tiger," she said, "the oldest and scariest tiger in the land."

On her way, the mother met an old woman who was very hungry. She gave the old woman all the food she had. But the old woman was still hungry and wanted to eat her hand. The mother didn't know the old woman was really Grandaunt Tiger in disguise. So she offered her hand. The tiger swallowed it and continued on.

23

Grandaunt Tiger now knew the mother's two girls were home alone. She went to their house. "Open the door!" she called.

The younger sister thought their mother had returned. But the older one said, "Mother's voice is like a bell. This voice is hoarse. It is certainly not Mother."

Grandaunt Tiger left and went into the mountains. There she drank spring water to rinse her throat. She returned to the house and again called the girls to open the door.

The older sister was still cautious. "Stick your hand inside," she said. She felt the tiger's hand. "Mother's hand is not so coarse."

Grandaunt Tiger went into the field. She wrapped a potato leaf around her hand. She returned to the house and again stuck her hand inside. The girls felt the soft hand. This time they let her in.

"Mother's face does not have so many moles," the older sister said.

"I'm your mother's mother," the old woman said. The girls had never met their grandmother before, so they believed her. They let her sleep with them.

In the middle of the night, the older sister awoke. She heard the grandmother chewing. "I'm hungry too," she said. "What are you eating?"

A peanut," the old woman lied. She was really chewing on the younger sister's hand. "Here, take one."

When the girl put the finger to her mouth, she knew it was not a peanut. She realized her grandmother was Grandaunt Tiger in disguise.

"I have to go to the bathroom," the girl said.

"It's dark outside. I'll tie a rope around you so you don't get lost," the old woman said.

The girl scurried outside, untied the rope, and re-tied it to a water pail. When the girl didn't return, the old woman pulled the rope. In came the pail. Furious, she ran outside, but she couldn't find the girl.

As the sun rose, the old woman saw the girl's shadow. "Come down!" she ordered.

"I know you want to eat me, Grandmother," the girl said. "I will let you. But first I want to eat some fried birds. Will you bring me some boiling oil?"

29

The old woman agreed. She brought out a wok filled with hot oil and a rope so the girl could pull it up. The girl fried some birds and then said, "OK. I'm ready. Open your mouth, and I will jump in!"

The old woman closed her eyes and opened her mouth. The girl quickly poured the scalding oil into it. Immediately the old woman turned into Grandaunt Tiger and died.

Glossary

corset—a woman's tight, stiff undergarment worn to support or give shape to waist and hips

culture—a people's way of life, ideas, art, customs, and traditions

ogress—a female monster or giant that eats peop.e; the male version is called an ogre

pelt—an animal's skin with the fur still on it

sifter—a device used to get rid of lumps from a substance such as flour

wok—a panlike bowl that is used for stir-frying food

Critical Thinking Using the Common Core

Find unique cultural elements of each story. How do these elements fit each culture or country? [Integration of Knowledge and Ideas]

Compare and contrast the three villains (the wolf, the ogress, and the tiger). How are they alike in each of the stories? How are they different? [Key Ideas and Details]

The Little Red Riding Hood character makes choices in each of the stories. How do these choices affect what happens in each story? [Craft and Structure]

Writing Prompts

1) Write a Little Red Riding Hood story set in your neighborhood. Use details that help identify your neighborhood (e.g., streets, parks, stores or buildings, people, clothing).

2) Choose one of the three stories and rewrite it as one of the characters. For example, tell Little Red Riding Hood's stcry as if you were the wolf.

Read More

Laird, Elizabeth. *The Ogress and the Snake and Other Stories from Somalia*. Folktales from Around the World. London: Frances Lincoln Children's Books, 2009.

Shaskan, Trisha Speed. *Honestly, Red Riding Hood Was Rotten!: The Story of Little Red Riding Hood as Told by the Wolf*. Mankato, Minn.: Picture Window Books, 2012.

Yolen, Jane. *Grumbles from the Forest: Fairy-Tale Voices with a Twist: Poems*. Honesdale, Penn.: WordSong, 2013.

Internet Sites

FactHound offers a safe, fun way to find Internet sites related to this book. All of the sites on FactHound have been researched by our staff.

Here's all you do:

Visit *www.facthound.com*

Type in this code: 9781479554355

Super-cool stuff! Check out projects, games and lots more at **www.capstonekids.com**

Thanks to our advisers for their expertise and advice:

Maria Tatar, PhD, Chair, Program in Folklore & Mythology
John L. Loeb Professor of Germanic Languages & Literatures and Folklore & Mythology
Harvard University

Terry Flaherty, PhD, Professor of English
Minnesota State University, Mankato

Editor: Jill Kalz
Designer: Ashlee Suker
Art Director: Nathan Gassman
Production Specialist: Katy LaVigne
The illustrations in this book were created digitally.

Picture Window Books are published by Capstone,
1710 Roe Crest Drive, North Mankato, Minnesota 56003
www.capstonepub.com

Library of Congress Cataloging-in-Publication Data
Gunderson, Jessica, author.
  Little Red Riding Hood stories around the world : 3 beloved tales / by Jessica Gunderson.
    pages cm. – (Nonfiction picture books. Multicultural fairy tales)
  Summary: Retells the classic German version of the fairy tale of a girl and a wolf, along with similar tales from Italy and Taiwan.
  ISBN 978-1-4795-5435-5 (library binding)
  ISBN 978-1-4795-5451-5 (paperback)
  ISBN 978-1-4795-5443-0 (paper over board)
  ISBN 978-1-4795-5459-1 (eBook PDF)
1. Fairy tales. 2. Folklore–Germany. [1. Fairy tales. 2. Folklore.]
I. Little Red Riding Hood. English. II. Title.
PZ8.G95Li 2015
398.2–dc23   2014006198

Printed in the United States of America in North Mankato, Minnesota.
102017   010892R

Look for all the books in the series:

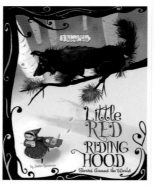